LOCAL FAUNA

Wick Poetry Chapbook Series Five
Catherine Wing, Editor

Poppy Seeds
Allison Davis

Here Both Sweeter
Daniel Carter

I Left My Wings on a Chair
Karen Schubert

Determinant
Alex Fabrizio

Local Fauna
Brian Brodeur

Little Nest
Diana Lueptow

LOCAL FAUNA

Poems by Brian Brodeur

The Kent State University Press
Kent, Ohio

Ohio Arts Council
A STATE AGENCY
THAT SUPPORTS PUBLIC
PROGRAMS IN THE ARTS

The Wick Poetry Series is sponsored in part by the Wick Poetry Center at Kent State University.

Cataloging information for this title is available at the Library of Congress.

for Anna

I was even accustomed to make an irruption into some houses, where I was well entertained, and after learning the kernels and very sieve-ful of news, what had subsided, the prospects of war and peace, and whether the world was likely to hold together much longer, I was let out through the rear avenues, and so escaped to the woods again.

—Thoreau, "The Village," *Walden*

CONTENTS

ACKNOWLEDGMENTS

The author wishes to thank the editors of the following periodicals in which these poems, sometimes in different versions, first appeared: *Crab Orchard Review:* "Blight"; *Eleven Eleven:* "For the Cigarette Holes in a Favorite Robe"; *Measure:* "Dear Proserpina"; *River Styx:* "Cousins"; *Shenandoah:* "A Stand of Swamp Maples in Purcellville, Virginia"; *The Southern Review:* "The Harbor" (from "Homeric Variations"); and *32 Poems:* "The Register" and "Young Achilles" (from "Homeric Variations").

"A Stand of Swamp Maples in Purcellville, Virginia" was featured on Poetry Daily on October 21, 2013. "Cousins" won third place in the 2012 *River Styx* International Poetry Contest as well as a 2012 Academy of American Poets Prize. "Photograph of Jack Spicer Holding a Life-Sized Bust of the Head of Jack Spicer" won a 2009 Dorothy Sargent Rosenberg Poetry Prize.

Grateful acknowledgment is made to the following teachers, colleagues, and friends who provided invaluable feedback on many of these poems: Lisa Ampleman, Eric Bliman, Don Bogen, Michelle Y. Burke, Danielle Cadena Deulen, James Cummins, John Drury, Claudia Emerson, Daniel Groves, Terrance Hayes, Brian Heston, Andrew Hudgins, Peter Klappert, Maurice Manning, Eric Pankey, Michael C. Peterson, Linwood Rumney, Steve Scafidi, J.D. Scrimgeour, Jack Snyder, Kevin Stoy, Chris Tanseer, and the members of the Portland Accord: Jessica Anthony, Benjamin Chadwick, Paul Rutz, and Max Stinson (who provided the title of this volume). Thanks are also owed to the English Department at University of Cincinnati for a George Elliston Fellowship in Poetry, *The Cincinnati Review,* and Nicola Mason, as well as the Sewanee Writers' Conference for a 2013 Walter E. Dakin Fellowship in Poetry.

The author also wishes to thank Peter Campion for choosing this manuscript as the winner of the 2013 Wick Poetry Center Student Competition, as well as David Hassler, Catherine Wing, Mary Young, and the rest of the staff of the Wick Poetry Center and the Kent State University Press for the excellent work they do to promote poetry.

Finally, the author acknowledges his family: Mark and Regina Brodeur, Erin Deslauriers, Courtney Brodeur, and his dear wife Kiley Cogis Brodeur without whose love and support none of these poems would have been possible. This chapbook is dedicated to their daughter Anna Constance Brodeur, the author's own faunal contribution, who was born two days before he learned he'd won the Wick Prize.

PHOTOGRAPH OF JACK SPICER HOLDING A LIFE-SIZED BUST OF THE HEAD OF JACK SPICER

Hair greased back, half-hidden from the camera,
he opens his mouth to kiss his own stone lips.

Does the stone kiss back? Its cold weight seems to lean
in anticipation, acquiescing to the thumb stroking

its ear, the familiar nose approaching, the living fist
tightening around the statue's throat.

From the look of strained affection on both faces,
anything could've passed between them.

Think of those lines composed just before he died:
A song, he wrote, *which I shall never sing*

has fallen asleep on my lips. Puckered or pursed,
neither figure hints at what happened next,

how long the two remained by the wainscoting,
waiting, I imagine, for the other to speak.

VIGIL

We were awakened Last night by a Servant desiring that I Should rise & Dress
to accompany Mrs P. to a Dying Neighbor's house, [. . .] I had the displea-
sure of keeping his body's Company the remainder of the night [. . .] I Made
a good Sketch of his head and Left the House[.]
   —J. J. Audubon, *Mississippi River Journal,* August 1, 1821

My Dearest Friend—
            I haven't slept in days,
& write to share the source of my Unrest.
When I arrived at James O'Connor's chamber
to sketch a deathbed portrait Sunday last,

I was too Late,—the poor man had expired.
I set to work dispersing onlookers,
fearing another Evasion of my fee,
& sat beside him with my Chalk and Paper.

Out of Nervousness, I introduced myself,—
I had not met him on my explorations
of the Parish, so Attendant was I
on Miss Eliza's French and Drawing lessons.

I asked if I could take the Liberty
of tucking his arms under the soiled sheets
to make him at least *look* more comfortable,
but his body Resisted my efforts.

In my Agitated state, I half-expected
a protestation, & stared into the blackness
of his unbreathing mouth, his eyes aglaze.
I said my Purpose: to impart a likeness

of him *approaching* death, pallid in aspect,
but Living still, if only feebly,—

& endeavored to contrive the Image of
a figure slipping into easeful sleep.

I closed his jaw, & heard the teeth click shut.
It was so queer to be thusly employed
by the One laid out before me,—to scrutinize
the Tuber of his nose, bulbous, empurpled.

I asked him to forgive my humble way
of speaking, explaining through my teeth:
It's always been my Nature, harsh or mild,
to favor Fact over propriety,

to render what I see, the visible
and what lies Underneath the visible.
His eyes, still wide, reflected candlelight:
dark berries Overripe inside his skull.

Dear Lucy, in our Thirteen Years together
we haven't much discussed the proposition
of Paradise, how you *envision* it.
I imagine the streets of Carlisle, England,

clamorous & thronged with human Commerce
as we roam the thoroughfares, admiring
the Great Breadth of the place: cobbled footways,
high city walls, a castle Towering,—

the Stateliness of the *tout Ensemble*
gleaming after a shower has washed clean
the public grounds, the landscape, & the Sea
swelling beyond, its surges murmuring.

In the bedchamber, I heard a scuttling—
the ladies Downstairs organizing breakfast.

Dawn steeped in the dark Beyond the casements
where rooky oaks, draped with Spanish moss,

rattled at the panes to be let in,—
I lit another candle, crumpling
the sketch I'd Labored over for an hour,
prepared a fresh sheet, & Began again.

NOT VERSED IN COUNTRY THINGS

I was thirty before I saw a living fox.
Clearing a gap in the chain-link, he darted out
and skittered across the road into a dirt lot,
and I thought, *What have I done to be so lucky?*

I watched his gauzy tail, his short legs trotting
as he splashed through puddles in tire tracks
and turned his head as if to acknowledge me
before he slipped into a clotted woods.

Whenever I passed that spot, I'd look for him,
glancing over my shoulder out the driver's side—
I'd look back at the road, glancing again,
until I almost clipped a girl on a bike.

Once, I parked beside the old post office
where crepe myrtle blossoms littered the berm
and flecked the asphalt pink. The car locks chirped.
I heard a sudden rustling in the grass.

From a swale of chicory, his white paws flashed.
How long had he been watching me?
Backlit, he nudged forward. I was so close
I could see his eyelashes as he blinked.

I didn't move. His ears perked up, his muzzle
opened to expose the pegs of his teeth
as he yipped, flicked his tail, and padded off,
a tuft of bent weeds swaying where he'd stood.

COUSINS

for David Brodeur (1976–2011)

1.

Last night, after the Air Force official
told your folks what happened to you in Kabul,

your brother called. I almost didn't answer.
The bullet to the face, which you survived,

pierced one cheek, he said, then the other,
but you rose from the floor and staggered after

the man who'd shot you, grabbing for his hand
as a second bullet severed your spinal cord.

I was going to say it was too much to hear
but I didn't have the right—you weren't *my* brother.

He called you a hero, asked if I had any questions.
"Questions?" I said, and he hung up the phone.

2.

It was rare to get the three of us together.
When you flew into DC, we drove to Skyline Drive

in separate cars, and hiked the Whiteoak Trail
to see if the falls were running. They were dry.

On the gravel path, fresh piles of horse dung
swarmed with monarchs and swallowtails

who feasted on something they'd found there.
For a long time we watched their wings

opening and closing in the hot wind,
their bodies pulsing with what resembled

pleasure, their legs and forked tails trembling,
their abdomens thick as pinky fingers.

3.
I don't know why I'm telling this to you.
You were there. You saw the butterflies, the view

of the Shenandoah Valley from the falls.
Draining my water bottle, I coughed and wheezed,

promised to join the gym and quit smoking.
Your brother walked ahead. You stayed behind.

We parted at the lot—I can't remember
if we shook hands before we found our cars.

In my rearview, the sun blazed off your hood,
slices of light flashing as you entered.

Your windshield glinted as if lit from within.
It hurt to look at you is what I mean.

FORCE

Ringling Bros. and Barnum & Bailey,
George Mason University, April 2009

In the Patriot Center lot, a crowd gathers
to watch Upali, an Asian elephant cow,
give rides to undergrads for twenty dollars.
Her trainer shouts for her to come, and throws
his ankus at her, striking the steel wire
that pens her in, and jabs her gray flanks
with a bullwhip: "*Rangu*—lift trunk."

What little force it takes to keep her tame.
Two girls mount up, and grab her tuft of hair
as the trainer yells, "*Diup*," and calls her name.
Sticking his hook in her mouth, he tugs at her,
and cries, "Move now, you move." She jolts the wicker
carriage, which makes the girls jostle and scream.
The trainer laughs, applauding as they scream.

TALK OF THE NATION

A student, Naema, calls from Kalamazoo,
and tells the authors of the featured book
that when she studied the triangle trade in school

she imagined a continent populated
by slaves: children literally born in cages,
who waited for their masters to claim them.

In the green light of the dash, my wife snorts,
a sound she makes whenever she hears
a statement so absurd it might be true,

and the esteemed professor emeritus from Hull
admits Naema's right, though only partly,
citing the countless thousands taken captive

by rival tribes (endemic ethnic warfare),
how they worked the land of their enemies
and were sold for rifles, rum, calico.

"For *real?*" Naema says. She sounds so young.
Her voice has a raspy aspect as she questions
why Africans would enslave their own people,

and the coauthors explain her misconception:
Africans didn't know they were African
until the Portuguese and Dutch arrived.

"Did *you* know that?" my wife asks, leering.
"Which part?" I say, "The stuff about the Dutch?"
"All of it," she says, "That can't be true."

"Sure it's true," I say, though it's new to me:
the rival tribes, the Dutch, the calico,
the way the Hull professor's tone of stern

authority makes me sneer at my wife's
disbelief instead of conceding my own.
The host of the show thanks his guests and sponsors,

and, as Naema says, "Excuse me, Sir,"
he cuts her off. My wife flips on the headlights.
"You must be right," she says. The theme song plays.

LOCAL FAUNA

1.

From the canopy of the Primate Jungle Trail,
they hooted their duets: deep tuneful trills
quavering through the day for food or love
above the traffic din on Clifton Ave.
It took a month to figure out those yowls
were gibbons at the Cincinnati Zoo.

We learned the names of Tom and Genie, too,
because we heard them brawl across the hall.
The first time Genie stumbled up the stairs
and pounded on our door, "He's got a knife!"
we let her in, and locked the bolt. Her hair
slick with sweat, she thanked us, hugged my wife.

But when I started dialing, she screamed,
"They're coming, Tom!" and took off after him.

2.

One night, I woke to thunder. As it passed,
I heard a clattering in the living room,
and bungled out of bed without my glasses.
On the office wall, a man's shadow loomed.

I chose my weapon: a hardback *Leaves of Grass*.
"Who's there?" I said, and lunged, stubbing my toe
as I grabbed for the man who dove across
the room toward an open office window.

I slammed my head against the still-closed frame.
My wife flipped on the light:
                              "Honey, what's wrong?"

Stunned, I rubbed my temples, "Fucking Tom."

"Fuck *who?*"
       "He must've wanted our widescreen."

Squinting at my reflection in the pane,
I laughed—the burglar's shadow had been mine.

3.
Walking up the bridge to Gibbon Island,
we saw a pair of Siamang males dangle
from iron bars assembled through the trees.
Thick-armed, wiry, they bantered and swung,
their huge throat sacks ballooning as they howled.
The bigger male pursued the smaller one
until the bigger stopped to cough and wheeze,
and the other squawked at him, rubbing it in.

At the far end of the bridge, a couple embraced,
feeding each other chunks of funnel cake.
They looked like Tom and Genie, but well-dressed.
"It *is* them," my wife said, turning away.
Tom tossed some cake toward the gibbon cage,
and Genie laughed. He bowed his head. They kissed.

4.
We hadn't heard the gibbons call for weeks.
I searched the internet for info on
primate depression—maybe they were sick.
Nothing. I asked my wife.
                    "Primate depression?
You're kidding, right?"
                    "We're primates, too, you know."

"I know, but we're—our brains are more evolved."

"I guess."

"Of course they are. Monkeys will throw
their own feces at you."
                    "But they feel love
and grief and rage like us."
                         "What do *you* know?
Primate depression. I bet they're inside
their winter quarters for the year."
                              "Sounds right."

I pictured heated cages where they'd squat
to gnaw each other's fur and lounge on beds
inlaid with leaves flown in from Borneo.

5.
From behind her locked door, Genie threatened
to call the cops, but Tom kept smashing his fist
on the knocker, screaming, "Bitch, you let me in!"
My wife and I took turns at the peephole.
The gash on his knuckles trickled down his wrist.
Then he started to weep, caressing the wall.
"Genie?" he pleaded, almost singing the word—
"You let me in? Please, Genie? No or yes?"

As soon as the sirens whined outside, he bolted.
Four flashlights streamed across the backyard lawn
until they found him hiding in the shed.
My wife untied my robe, sliding her hands
along my chest. "Let's go to bed," she said.
I squirmed against her touch: "Your hands are cold."

BLIGHT

Worcester, MA

I was born in a city with a river running beneath it.
Summers, the chemical stink of textile dyes
seeped up from viaducts under the streets.
Two bridges spanned a lake to the northeast
that fed into the river underground.
We heard of those who walked the bridges at night
and climbed guardrails, who scaled trestles
to leap into the water and disappear.
We heard a lot of things: the newborn boy
dumped in a Papa Gino's ladies room,
the ServiceMaster van with painted windows
parked by the playground woods, two teenage girls
found naked in a ditch near Great Brook Valley
where we were told never to go after dark.
Bored, we'd steal fresh cemetery flowers,
and pitch them at each other, shattering
blooms with a bat that gave us special power
because we'd heard Yastrzemski owned it once.
Sticky with strips of black electrical tape,
it belonged to Joe Camuso down the street.
When Joe showed up one day without the bat,
he said his dad had split it beating a man
he'd caught that morning pissing on their stoop.
"Dad wasn't even drunk," Joe said, grinning.
Police tape fluttered there until it tattered.
The night Joe's dad got off on self-defense,
my own father staggered home after the party
at Stoney's Bar, waking my stepmother.
I heard the thud of boots dropped on the floor,
voices murmuring through the drywall.
"I'm sick of all these Blacks," he said. She shushed him:
"Quiet, the kids will hear." "Sorry," he said,
"I mean these *African Americans*."

CINCINNATI PASTORAL

1.

She liked running alone through the park at dusk,
the cold making her wheeze, the dark erasing
the trees along the trail as the first stars
stippled the winter sky above the city.

In Burnet Woods, she climbed the stone steps
off Brookline Avenue, veered down a path
through saplings clattering like music stands,
and took a road she didn't recognize.

As she approached a car—a black LeSabre
parked on the curb—she noticed spits of rain
spattering the windshield, one wiper blade
smearing drops, the other missing.

She looked at the sky, the gray light draining,
then glanced into the passenger side:
a man behind the wheel, his fly
open, his fist stuffed down his jeans.

He leaned over the console, gaped at her.
Hearing the engine rattle into gear, she turned
to see his taillights glowing up the hill,
and thought, Okay, *that's* over.

*

On the park's steepest climb, a car's high beams
blinded her. She tried to keep her footing
but she slipped on slush and tumbled down
a gully, her body clipping boulders and trunks of trees,

her glasses flinging off as her shoulder
smashed a retaining wall with a cracking sound.
She heard a car door slam at the top of the hill.
A man's voice calling. "I'm fine," she said.

How far had she fallen? "Hold on," he shouted.
She thought she heard a belt buckle jangling.
Feeling for her glasses, she touched what felt like
a brick, and gripped it tightly, listening.

From the way he seemed to gallop down the slope,
holding both arms out, he must've tripped
or slipped on the slick incline, stumbling down
the gulley into the wall. "Hello?" she said.

She poked him with the brick. He grunted, kicked.
Dead leaves and ice stuck to his frayed dreadlocks.
Groping out of the ditch, she staggered toward
the lights on Ludlow, still carrying the brick.

2.
This was 2001, before the riots that April
when police fired teargas at men and women
demanding answers from the City Council
after the Thomas shooting in Over-the-Rhine.

They set small fires, looted, shot handguns.
No one died. Safe in the Gaslight District,
she watched the news with other UC students,
and vowed, because she could, to never go back.

Why did she conflate these different places?
Burnet Woods, downtown, Over-the-Rhine—
they just seemed *other* to her, dangerous—
She might not leave her studio again.

Then summer came. She passed the swings, the hill.
Peering into the woods for a break in the thicket,
she climbed down what looked like an old deer trail,
scooting on her butt. Nothing seemed right.

The slope wasn't steep enough, the pricker bushes
dwarfed and ragged, choked with leaves.
The wall, too short, crumbled at her touch.
Thick undergrowth buried the ground with green.

RETURNS

There is no innocent explanation.
   —Bernard Madoff, 12/11/2008

Relieved when they arrested me, I slumped
in the back of the cruiser with my head

between my knees, and smiled—
I didn't have to lie anymore.

Even being in lockdown was like a vacation.
I was free. The inmates all knew me.

"Hey, Bernie," they'd say, "how'd you steal
that money from those old Jewish ladies?"

"Fuck them," I'd say, "I floated them for years.
If anything, *I'm* the victim here."

Why should I be ashamed? My life's over.
Or else it's just begun—either way.

It doesn't change the fact my son is dead.
The day I heard, I was walking the track

when a guard told me I had a visitor.
Through the Plexiglas, I saw Ruth had been crying.

I buttoned up my standard-issue khaki shirt,
sat at the booth that stank of disinfectant,

and lifted the receiver to my ear. . . .
It's not what he did, but how he did it.

I picture him driving to Home Depot
for a length of rope, and waiting for the kids

to fall asleep before he wrote his note,
kicking away the office chair.

He made his choice—I know it's not my fault.
I called him once last year before the trial

to tell my side, how I'd been used,
and how I'd never lie to family.

He didn't speak, but he was listening.
I could hear him breathing at the other end.

VARIATIONS ON A THEME BY BORGES

Lo matan y no sabe que muere para que se repita una escena.

1. *The Stunt Double*

He'll parachute for you, or take a bullet.
He'll snorkel through a shark tank thick with chum,
cleaning his wounds as you enter the shot
in time to kiss the girl and snag the ransom.

Would you treat him with kindness or disdain?
Flushed one night with the feeling that your life
was never yours, you call him to complain
about your dream of driving off a cliff.

Pinned between the seat and steering column,
you howl for him to take your place instead.
Glass everywhere. The reek of gasoline.

He stoops to strike a match against your chin.
You die, he says, *but you don't know you're dead,
so that the scene can be played out again.*

2. *The Reenactors*

   North Bridge, Lexington, MA, 2010

Call it a boys club, hicks playing dress-up—
Our kids have said much worse under their breath.
Stowing our smartphones down our buckskin trousers,
we clink canteens, and swear, "Nothing like war
to bring us all together." And it's fun.
When Redcoats swarm the lot and form their lines,
we aim into the fog at friends and neighbors
without fear of the cops (they're Regulars).

But it's the blood we love to love, the cries,
the sting of musket fire in our eyes
as we lumber down the green in buckle shoes
to snare drums rattling and cannon salutes.
Who wins, who loses, who lives and dies:
Today, at least, we can predict our lives.

HOMERIC VARIATIONS

1. *Young Achilles*

Bored of playing swords, barefaced Achilles
trundles down the dunes at Skyros Harbor
to search the shoreline for washed-up debris.
He watches a man work a spit into a mackerel
and wipe gore from his knife on the rags he wears.
Why should *he* get to light fires on the beach
and swim in the ocean without a chaperone?
Achilles collects what stones he can carry,
and lobs the first, which splashes a tide pool
beside the man and spatters foam on his feet.
Squinting, the man turns to survey the dunes
as Achilles aims and fires another one.
He strikes the man's groin. The man collapses.
"I want you off my beach," Achilles screams.
"*Your* beach?" says the man. "That's right, my beach."
Achilles hurls one bigger than his fist.
"Yes!" he hisses. The man's brow bleeds—
he clasps his hands, asking for mercy, mercy.
Achilles smiles: Why shouldn't he be feared?
He wishes he could throw stones at the sea
and stop the senseless tide from always shifting.
The man has stopped moving. Achilles walks
toward the body to investigate,
and flips him on his back with his sandaled foot.
Close up, the man looks young. His skinny arms
could be a boy's arms twisted underneath him.
Sand fleas flick in and out of his mouth.
Careful not to step in the darkened mud,
tender-heeled Achilles bows to stroke
the man's wet face and hair, closing his eyes.
"There, there," he says, "that's better, go to sleep."

2. *The Harbor*

We rowed all afternoon and didn't speak.
When the beeswax in our ears dripped down our beards,
we heard the singing: women's voices trilling
a melody we knew but could not place.

We dropped our oars, and leaned against the gunwales,
looking toward the harbor dotted with rocks
where groggy seals barked and sprawled, their figures
frisking in the foam of combers breaking.

The song grew louder then, flooding the air
with strains that made our hearts beat in our ears.
Our pumping blood accompanied the music
it hurt to hear but hurt more not to hear.

The seals lifted their heads as if to catch
the song inside their mouths, their jaws gaping,
their sleek bodies bobbing to the rhythm,
swaying together in a kind of trance.

Misenus broke the spell, tossing the vat
of wax at our feet, pointing and glaring at us
until we pressed fresh clumps into our ears.
Our thoughts sounded like wind inside a shell.

Riding a long swell, we rose and fell
into open water, leaving behind the islands.
The surface of the sea glinted like fish scales.
The blades dipped in the waves, and scudded foam.

We wanted to *be* the seals, to feel our bellies
slap against cold stone, our wet fur gleaming—
We wanted to crack raw mussels with our teeth
and doze beside each other in the sun.

MRS. BAUMEISTER

The police came to me and said, "We are investigating your husband
in relation to homosexual homicide." [. . .] I remember saying to them,
"Can you tell me what homosexual homicide is?"
—Julie Baumeister, *People*, 12/23/1996

Thank you for seeing me on such short notice.
I've never had to hire a lawyer before,
and I don't think I really need one now.

Herb couldn't be the one who killed those boys.
The day our son brought home a human skull
he'd found behind our property, Herb said

it was the medical-school skeleton
his father, Dr. Baumeister, had owned.
Herb didn't know how else to dispose of it.

He's always been a conscientious man.
When Friesian foals we kept either broke free
or died, naturally, Herb was distraught.

He even bought a backhoe off a neighbor—
"There's one right tool for every job," he'd say.
Herb was under so much stress those days.

I blamed the Save-a-Lot we owned in Muncie.
Some weeks we wouldn't see him for three days.
He'd come home with dark bruises up his arms—

from restocking shelves, unloading trailer pallets—
and gripe about the college kids he'd hired.
"Don't you get sick," he'd spit, "of all these faggots?"

"What faggots?" I'd ask. He'd glare at me.
This was around the time *The Star* reported
the Strangler of I-70, the one

police thought picked up hitchhikers, young men
he had *relations* with before they died.
I told Herb not to leave the house at night.

I'd hear him in the kitchen with his keys
rattling in his fist. He'd set them down,
and pick them up again, rattling.

One morning, still dark, I woke to the odor
of woodsmoke, and found Herb's daybed empty.
Firelight went blinking through the trees.

In the backfield, he stood there in his boots,
just poking at the embers of a blaze
with a charred snow shovel. He was so sweaty.

I wanted to ask what he thought he was doing
outside without his coat, but I felt scared,
like I was interrupting, so I left.

I'm not *stupid*. But I have kids to raise.
My teaching job at New Joy Lutheran.
What could I say to make them understand?

Is that your wife and daughter on the desk?
Beautiful family. What would you do
if one of them—if you *suspected* something?

You'd fight to keep your family from harm.
If the wicked are rewarded, like Herb says,
all good people can do is find a place

to hide away and keep the world locked out.
He *couldn't* be the one. I don't believe
the things they say he did so many times.

How can you know a man twenty-three years
and not know him at all? Don't answer that.
I've taken too much of your day already.

LITTLE BESTIARY

1. *The Believer*

Feasting on blossoms, the gray squirrel scales
a horse chestnut to tear fresh panicles

from branches, holding each petal to the sun
before he gnaws and drops them on the lawn.

It looks like an ancient rite, some offering
to Spring, to the yellow orb warming his fur.

Why *can't* a gray squirrel wax devotional?
He clasps his claws tight around his meal

as if in prayer, and rasps asthmatic psalms
like a laryngitic child whose foot's been stomped.

Standing upright to reach the topmost limbs
and will the blowsy manna down to him,

he holds both hands aloft in supplication
for the bounty he's about to receive, amen.

2. *Rat Heaven*

> Rats don't ask for that much, really—a temple
> of their own, a few worshippers . . .
> —Dorothy Hoffman

Because they have "tickle skin," a flesh
on their bellies more sensitive to the touch,

and because they chirp when they're stroked,
tittering before meals or sex, an ultrasonic squeak

of rodent joy so faint we need transducers
to hear it, I imagine them looking down on us,

whole nests packing into celestial sewers
burrowed under Elysium's leafy bowers:

rat souls migrating toward a pale fluorescence
as they laugh about how happy they were once

to sniff at troughs of our earthly leavings,
to feast and fuck among our trash, thriving

as we thrived, how they once loved us
in ways that we could never love ourselves.

3. *Paper Wasps*

For weeks in May the queen shapes her saliva
into architecture, pulping bark and stem

for the brood she lays inside her open combs.
Teeming over each other, they throb and writhe,

their compound eyes vacant as a shark's.
When the air cools, their numbers dwindling,

some struggle in a spiderweb until they tire.
Because they have evolved to know their own—

the unique shapes of faces, mandibles—
I wonder if they pass each other and think:

What's the point? I check under the sill,
but I don't find their bodies anywhere.

Leaving the nest in tact through a long winter,
I watch in spring, and hope they won't return.

DEAR PROSERPINA

Ain't no sunshine when she's gone.
—Bill Withers

Maybe you're right. My love for you *is* cruel.
My late-night appetites and gifts that sparkle:
misogynistic—there's that word again.

In bed, I'd slip a finger underneath
your nightclothes to see if you were sleeping.
You always were. Except the night you muttered,

"Kill me, please," laughing a throaty wheeze
that startled me. I tried to comfort you.
You rose with a start, blinking, and looked at me

as if you'd never seen my face before.
I called your name, but you kept screaming, screaming
and clawing the air. I thought you'd never stop.

So often I misjudge these situations.
Through a tangle of candelabras and cloth flowers,
I'd watch you read a novel across the table.

I'd say, "I'm happy," and I'd force a smile.
"Me, too," you'd say, "Now let me finish eating."
And immediately I'd wish I'd said nothing,

that every utterance could be taken back,
the words spoken in anger, the tender things.
Sometimes your skin against mine feels so real

I don't know what to think, what I *should* feel.
I touch the fuzz on your belly. "Stop," you say,
"Quit it—you're tickling," and you turn away.

Last night, I wandered the halls, looking for . . .
What? I couldn't say. I thought I'd heard
a tune I used to know seep through the walls,

some old rondel, stiff and faintly martial.
I clapped my hands to make the music stop—
It only grew louder, and I was overcome

with the desire to dance, to stomp across the floor
and see my face reflected back at me
in polished stone. I romped until I tired.

I tried to recall the touch of you, your heat
when we first danced together years ago,
the sounds you made that night grinding your teeth

like stones gnashing together to make sparks.
I swear I smelled your perfume on the air,
the scent of calamus and coriander.

I scanned the chamber. How long had it been
since I'd visited this wing of the ancient house?
It tickled me to think you haven't seen

this space before. Long floral papering
still clinging as it tatters at the seams.
Years ago, I'd repair to this drawing room

to collect myself beside the fire. You see?
There *are* some things about me you don't know.
I want to take you there, to sit you down

and rub your freckled shoulders, hear you laugh,
and try to tell the difference between
your shrieks of pleasure and your cries of pain.

THE REGISTER

On the steps of the public library this morning,
I watch a man in waders pressure-wash the marble
glazed with a patina of pigeon shit.
Billows of frothy spray spew from his nozzle
as he flicks his wrist to increase the stream
and stares at a girl in spandex shorts
who chains her bike to the rack, unclips her helmet,
and shakes out her damp curls.

The man's radio blasts Weekend Edition:
Renee Montaigne and Steve Inskeep announcing
that four hundred years ago this week
Thomas Thorpe entered into the Stationer's Register
his right to print the first of Shakespeare's sonnets.
When listeners were asked, "What words of love
in our time could last as long?" they responded:
the songs of Kris Kristofferson, the rhymes of Fifty Cent. . . .

I'd like to enter into the Register
my desire to capture the way this man
grins at this girl, how he angles the pressure-washer
to mizzle the daylilies with spits of mist
as she ascends the steps, ignoring him
and the jets he spurts across the façade, bright bands
of yellow and indigo hanging in air
just long enough for a kid to yell, "Rainbow!"

FOR THE CIGARETTE HOLES IN A
FAVORITE ROBE

Indelible as knots in boards, most burns
stay on the surface, evidence

of some moment's carelessness
branded into the cloth. Like dwarf constellations

projected in negative, they punctuate
my chest—white sky, black stars.

Others go deep enough to show skin,
recalling what Henri Cartier-Bresson said

about the past, that it's tabula rasa
but sometimes it comes back like a burp.

Once, I thought I'd be the master
of my own plot, the boss of me.

Now, I'm happy to kill the garden lights,
and root around the phlox my wife planted,

and press my face to the dirt, listening
for the scuffle of night creatures in the understory.

It's not—it never was—the liberty
of breathing the rich mulch-smells of evening air

or feeling weeds licking my bare feet,
but roaming out to the edge of the property

and hearing a voice, so stern and familiar,
calling me, by name, to come inside.

A STAND OF SWAMP MAPLES IN PURCELLVILLE, VIRGINIA

From the window you can see which trees I mean.
I used to have a view for twenty acres
of pine and poplar woods, a cattle pasture
where I'd see mother foxes with their kits.

Now, only these dozen trees divide me
from townhouses sprouting from the hills.
Rotten to the root, they won't survive,
their branches webbed with fat silk-moth cocoons.

When I called Pro Arbor Tree Service in Reston,
an agent asked to take my information
and told me he could send a crew next Tuesday.
I hung up without leaving my number.

I'm glad I thought of you and glad you came.
With my bursitis, I can't do much these days.
Strong enough last week to tug the pull cord
of my saw, I walked across the woodyard,

and breathed the blue fumes the chainsaw belched,
and listened to it shriek as I touched the teeth
to the sickliest tree. I had to stop myself.
I wasn't up to it, but now you're here.

Take the woodshed keys. The saw's gassed up.
I see you brought your old Dodge Power Wagon.
Haul all the wood you need. I don't want money.
Just leave a quarter cord behind for me.